Mommy and Daddy Are Always Supposed to Say Yes . . . Aren't They?

Written by B. Annye Rothenberg, Ph.D.
Child/Parent Psychologist

Illustrated by Marion Eldridge

REDWOOD CITY, CALIFORNIA

DEDICATION

This book is dedicated to my mother and father, my grandmother, and my uncle, for all you've done – and most especially to my son Bret for being all that you are and for all that you do.   — B.A.R.

To Mom and Dad, with love.   — M.E.

Text copyright © 2007 by B. Annye Rothenberg
Illustrations copyright © 2007 by Marion Eldridge

Library of Congress Cataloging-in-Publication Data

Rothenberg, B. Annye, 1940-
  Mommy and daddy are always supposed to say yes-- aren't they? / B. Annye Rothenberg, illustrated by Marion Eldridge. -- 1st ed.
        p. cm.
  Publication includes children's book and a parent's guide in one.
  "Alex expects to always have his way and learns why that can't be; and a guide for parents teaches how much control preschoolers need in order to have high self-esteem" -- Provided by publisher.
  ISBN-13: 978-0-9790420-0-3 (pbk.)
  ISBN-10: 0-9790420-0-3 (pbk.)
  1. Parenting. 2. Self-esteem in children--Juvenile literature. I. Eldridge, Marion, ill. II. Title.
  HQ755.8.R676 2007
  649'.64--dc22

                          2006039002

Printed in China   First printing May, 2007
10 9 8 7 6 5 4 3 2 1

REDWOOD CITY, CALIFORNIA

**Published by
Perfecting Parenting Press**
www.perfectingparentingpress.com

Book design by
Cathleen O'Brien
San Francisco, California

Children's book in collaboration with
SuAnn and Kevin Kiser
Palo Alto, California

Parents' Guide edited by
Caroline Grannan
San Francisco, Calforina

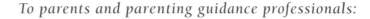

To parents and parenting guidance professionals:

• HOW TO USE THIS BOOK •

This book focuses on the dilemma of **how to raise children to be capable, confident, content, and empathetic**, in an era when parents are encouraged to give their children a lot of control, often overindulging them. The **first part** of this book is a **story for young children ages three through five**. The **second part** is **a comprehensive guidance section for parents** (as well as those who guide parents, such as pediatricians and preschool teachers). Together, these two parts help both child and parents better understand why Mommy and Daddy can't always say yes.

In the children's story, a young boy named Alex expects his parents to give him what he wants and allow him to do whatever he wants. During the course of the story, Alex comes to realize that his personal wishes are not the only ones that matter. His parents want him to understand why they can't always let him have his way. They help him to learn that when they say no, it doesn't mean they don't love him – quite the opposite.

Read the children's story to yourself first. Then as you read it out loud, ask your young listener if the events in the story happen at home – and when they do, what happens? "Does Mommy ever say that to you?" "What does Daddy do when you say that?" "How come Alex did that?" "Do you ever do that?" The story helps you teach all these lessons and lays the foundation for you to continue to point out examples to your child in the future.

The Parents' Guide helps you look at the issues raised in Alex's story and **re-evaluate your approach to child-rearing**. The Introduction **and** Section One explain why parents are uncertain about how to build their child's self-esteem, what your child's capabilities are, how preschoolers think, and why parents often have control conflicts with their preschoolers. Section Two helps you develop a parenting approach that builds your child's self-esteem while teaching him what your role is in raising him – and what his role is. It helps you take the lead. You'll learn strategies for addressing child-rearing differences with your spouse so you can work together toward your parenting goals. In Section Three, you'll learn about the important, age-appropriate, and reasonable rules for preschoolers. You'll begin to see if your child is learning what he needs to from the choices you give him and the limits you set.

The guide includes case studies – examples from families of preschoolers – and **concludes with a summary of practical guidelines**. If your time is very limited, you can read the summary on pages 37-38 and go back later and read the complete guide for a fuller understanding of these issues concerning your child and yourself.

— *Annye Rothenberg, Ph.D., Child/Parent Psychologist*

My name is Alex. My favorite day is Sunday, because Mommy and Daddy and I spend the whole day together. We don't have to rush and we do lots of fun things.

One Sunday, Daddy was making breakfast. "Do you want French toast or pancakes?" he asked.

"I'd love French toast," said Mommy.

"I don't want French toast," I said. "And I don't want pancakes. I want waffles with syrup."

"We don't have any waffles," said Daddy. "Alex, remember how much you liked the French toast with syrup we had last Sunday?"

"I only want waffles with syrup!" I yelled.

"Honey, there just aren't any," said Daddy. "But shouting isn't a good way to tell us things."

I wanted Daddy to let me have what I wanted for breakfast. I think there should be waffles in the freezer. Mommy could have gone to the store to get them. Mommy and Daddy should always give me what I want ... *shouldn't they?*

After a while, my stomach started to growl. I felt very hungry.

"Can I please have breakfast?" I asked.

"That's a nice way to ask, Alex," said Mommy. "Come and sit at the table. There's enough French toast for everybody."

"I'm glad we're all having breakfast together," Daddy said.

I ate my French toast with syrup,

and it was yummy in my tummy

7

After breakfast, I heard someone laughing outside. I went to the window. Some big kids were playing ball.

"Alex, please bring me your plate," said Mommy. "I'm going to wash the dishes now."

"In a minute," I said. "I'm busy."

"I don't want to have to ask you again," said Mommy.

I wanted to watch the kids play ball. I think Mommy and Daddy should just let me do what I want ... *shouldn't they?*

I kept watching the kids and I didn't bring Mommy my plate.

"You're not listening," said Mommy. "Please bring your plate, Alex. I'm waiting!"

I didn't think Mommy was being nice. But I brought her my plate because I don't like it when she's unhappy with me.

After a little while, Mommy said, "Is everyone ready for our walk to the pond?"

"I'll get some bread to feed the ducks," said Daddy.

I love feeding the ducks, so I got ready fast.

"I want to carry the bread," I said.

Daddy gave me the big bread bag. We started on our walk. It was a hot day and soon I got tired of walking.

"Mommy," I said, "carry me."

"You have to walk, Alex," said Mommy. "You're getting to be a big boy."

"**No**, I'm not a big boy," I said. "I **can't** walk. It's too hot and I'm too tired."

"Of course you can walk," said Daddy. "I'll race you to the corner!"

"I don't want to race," I said. "Mommy, you have to carry me. I won't be your friend if you don't carry me."

Mommy frowned. "I'm sorry this walk is so hard for you," she said. "But I won't carry you."

That didn't make me happy. Mommy and Daddy are always supposed to make me happy ... *aren't they?* I sat down right on the ground and dropped the bag of bread.

"I **won't** walk," I said.

"We're almost there," said Daddy. "The ducks will be so glad to have some bread to eat." He picked up the bread bag.

I didn't get up.

"We'll try to save some bread for you to feed the ducks," said Mommy.

I still didn't get up.

Then Mommy and Daddy started walking slowly. When they got to the corner, I jumped up and ran after them.

"Wait for me," I shouted.

We all walked together the rest of the way to the duck pond. When we got there, we took turns feeding the ducks. They quacked and pushed each other out of the way. We all laughed.

"That was fun," I said.

On the way home, Mommy and Daddy whispered to each other. I couldn't hear what they said. Then Mommy gave me a funny kind of smile and said, "Do you know what, Alex? I'm tired of being in charge."

"I am too," said Daddy. "Alex, would you like to be the boss?"

"I can be the boss?" I asked. "I can be in charge?"

"Yes," said Mommy and Daddy.

"OK!" I said. "Wow, I'm in charge!"

As we walked home, Mommy said, "I want my bicycle."

"Your bicycle is at home," I said in a very grown-up voice.

Mommy said, "But I want it now."

"You have to walk home first," I said. "Then you can have it."

"No," said Mommy.

Mommy sure wanted things her way. She wanted her bicycle right now. I didn't know what to do about that. So we kept walking.

Then Daddy said, "There are some pretty flowers in that yard. I'm going to pick them."

"No," I said. "You can't just pick other people's flowers."

"But I want them," said Daddy.

"You have to think of other people — not just yourself," I said in my very best grown-up voice.

"I don't want to think about other people," said Daddy.

"Being the boss isn't much fun," I said. "Nobody can just have whatever they want whenever they want it."

"But grown-ups are always supposed to say yes to their children," said Mommy, "...*aren't they*?"

"No," I said. "That's not right."

"And children don't have to think about what's good for other people," said Daddy, "...*do they*?"

"Of course they do," I said. "Otherwise, they aren't being nice."

"We wanted you to be in charge so you could learn those things," said Daddy. "But it sounds to me like you already know them."

"You are very smart, Alex," said Mommy. "And we love every bit of you, from the top of your hair to the bottom of your toes. From here all the way to the stars."

I giggled and we had a big family hug.

"Do you know what I feel like doing?" I said.

"What?" said Mommy.

"I can't even guess," said Daddy.

"Can we take out the little pool when we get home and fill it with water," I asked, "so we can get cool, just like the ducks in the pond?"

"And eat bread crumbs?" asked Daddy.

I laughed and said, "Not bread crumbs. Sandwiches."

"Yes!" Mommy and Daddy both said.

We had a fun day together.

Even though Mommy and Daddy can't always say yes to me, I still like it better when they do. But I know for sure they love me, even when they say no.

A GUIDE FOR PARENTS

• INTRODUCTION •

Most popular child-rearing books today encourage parents to make building their child's self-esteem their number-one goal. Parents are advised to give children of all ages – even toddlers – a lot of choices and "say." *However, many parents who have adopted this approach find their children becoming self-centered, spoiled, and less respectful of adults and other children.* Teachers complain about even very young children wanting their way, arguing with them, having no empathy toward others, and refusing to apologize. Parents are starting to question whether this approach is too permissive.

Many parents are becoming increasingly concerned about their children's behavior. Their children ignore, refuse, and negotiate with them, being rude and sometimes relentless unless things go their way. *It's hard for parents to be happy with a child who is pushing their boundaries all the time.* Parents become frustrated and angry with their children. As children sense this, their self-esteem decreases – resulting in an outcome exactly the opposite from what their parents hoped for. While parents want high self-esteem for their children, they wonder how to prevent these troublesome and unacceptable behaviors.

Most contemporary child-rearing books fail to explain that parents should give young children only a little bit of choice and say. As their age and life experience increase, children can be given more and more say – especially if you have helped them to become thoughtful decision-makers and problem-solvers instead of little royalty who expect to control everything in their lives.

Self-esteem does not develop because a child has a lot of choice and say. It blossoms when he[1] learns acceptable behavior so he doesn't need constant correction from others, and when he acquires sufficient competence that he doesn't feel less capable than his peers. *Self-esteem comes from developing competence in many areas,* generally in the following priority:

1. Learning to listen so that he knows how to behave without frequent reminders.
2. Developing age-appropriate skills such as language and motor skills.
3. Developing enough emotional security to feel comfortable and confident even when you're not always available to him.
4. Learning how to socialize capably with others.
5. Developing the appropriate self-help skills for his age, such as learning how to get dressed and clean up after himself.
6. Having age-appropriate choices and say – not too much and not too little.

Preschool children need to learn to accept their parents' decision-making as an essential foundation for developing high self-esteem. As they get older and develop more independence, children slowly gain ability to make more of the decisions for themselves. Limits help children know what to expect, so they can, with time, learn age-appropriate skills and behave acceptably and responsibly. Children feel good about themselves when they know they are capable and behaving well.

[1]To avoid the awkward use of he/she, the sections within this guide will alternate between both.

CASE STUDY:
A CHILD WITH TOO MUCH CONTROL LEADS TO AN OUT-OF-CONTROL CHILD

Julie and Bob's daughter Emma had become very strong-willed. Now, at four, she would become very angry whenever she didn't get her way. She would shout "No!" and berate her parents when they asked her to pick up her toys or when they added an extra errand to their shopping trip. "You're a bad Mommy!" "I don't like you, Daddy!" "You're not the boss of me!" Julie and Bob became increasingly concerned about her difficult and out-of-bounds behavior. They realized that they had been avoiding confrontations with Emma. They would let her have her way – and if that was impossible, they would apologize profusely or offer her something special like a toy, a piggyback ride, or a hug. They suspected that their reluctance to say no to Emma was encouraging her willfulness.

After a professional consultation, Julie and Bob realized that they were hampering her personality development by avoiding saying no to her. They explained to Emma that they would be making some changes that would help them all get along better as a family. With both parents working together, they began to insist that she do what they asked. Emma was very, very angry the first few days. When she got out of bounds, they redirected her, reminding her what she needed to do and giving her a reason or an incentive to cooperate: "You need to stop playing and get your shoes. If you can do it fast, we'll have time to stop at the playground." If that failed, they gave her an appropriate consequence, such as a time-out, no cooking with Mommy, or no TV.

They also helped her begin to understand her angry feelings and behavior. **They learned that the phrase "use your words" is too abstract for a preschooler** and instead offered specific phrases to help her express her anger in acceptable words and behavior: "You can say, 'I'm mad because I wanted to keep playing.' But it's not OK to hit me or say 'You're a stupid poopy head.' "

To help Emma become less self-centered, **they insisted that she phrase her requests politely:** *"Mommy (Daddy), when you have a minute, could you please…?"*

Within a few days, Emma began to use these tools. In a few weeks, she was reacting more reasonably when her parents said no. As she began to accept the inevitable no's, she became less relentless, angry, and mean.

Emma had been given too much control too soon, which encouraged her to fly into a rage when she couldn't have her way. By redirecting her anger and taking a confident and reasonable stand as parents, Julie and Bob helped Emma to accept and respect their important role as her limit-setting "gatekeepers." Best of all, Emma had become happier – a child who felt better about herself as her parents became happier with her. The following sections will fully explain how parents can make some changes needed in their own child-rearing strategies.

• SECTION ONE •
UNDERSTANDING YOUR CHILD
Why Children Test Limits

Young children are naturally curious, exploratory, and fun-loving. ***But, because of their age, they are also typically self-centered and impulsive, and therefore believe in their right to do what they want and have what they want whenever they want it – usually right now***. Although many of the things they want to do are reasonable, limits have to be set. You don't want them to throw the ball in the house, leave large messes for you to clean up, or ignore you. It is natural for young children to try out things you don't want them to do and resist doing some things you want them to do. Preschoolers (ages three through five) are often oppositional and say no to many of their parents' requests. This is not surprising, because their immediate goals are very different from those of adults.

Your child will learn early that you have rules that prevent her from doing whatever she wants. ***It is predictable that she will try to find ways to push you into saying yes***. Delaying bedtime, requesting treats, refusing to turn off the TV, and demanding more playtime are common examples. When you deny your child's demands, she can get frustrated and angry and can have tantrums. She may retort: "I'm going to anyhow." "You have to do what I say."

"If you don't let me watch cartoons, I won't be happy." "You're a mean Mommy." "I won't be your friend, Daddy."

Parents are often surprised and concerned at preschoolers' quick and dramatic emotional changes: from happy to silly, to furious, sad, or insecure, to happy and calm again. The swings are common at this age as children experience all kinds of feelings when things don't go their way. All this drama can make parents feel drained and angry, often for hours, while their child seems to recover much more quickly. This is when many parents want to shout: "It's not fair!"

However, children are motivated to please, and they love their parents' praise. Learning how to please you is the way your child becomes socialized over time. Some parents feel that they don't want to raise their children to have to please others, but even adults need to take others into consideration in what they say and do.

BECOMING A GOOD GATEKEEPER

Many parents are uncertain about what rules to set and whether they have enough or too few. Some parents are also uncomfortable about being the gatekeeper, being in charge all the time. They want their children to have a lot of say. However, this is where parents and children get into difficulty with each other, because parents also don't want their children to act like another parent in the family. Parents have a right and a responsibility to teach their children how to behave. You demonstrate this when you say, for example: "It's my job to teach you everything three-year-olds need to know about how to behave when we go out to dinner."

This phrase – "it's my job to teach you everything __-year-olds need to know" – is an important one for children to hear you say. As a parent seeking to set healthy limits, you'll need to learn what is and isn't reasonable and developmentally appropriate for your child's age. Remember that many developmental changes happen from three to five years of age, and that there is a lot of variation among children.

A preschooler *should* be expected to do things such as:

- learn to play by himself for at least 15 minutes, many times a day
- do most of the work in picking up his toys
- be able to listen to storybooks and ask and answer questions about them
- respond to what you say and not ignore you
- be mostly or completely toilet-trained
- wash and dry his own hands
- feed himself with a fork and spoon
- use "please" and "thank you"
- be mostly able to share and take turns with peers

A preschooler *should not* be expected to do things such as:

- always immediately obey what you say no matter how you say it
- be logical when upset
- communicate clearly when upset or "use his words" without your help
- be efficient when helping you with chores
- have the same appetite from day to day
- always be happy to go to preschool or child care
- resolve most conflicts with other children
- cross the street by himself

Learning how much to expect of your preschooler can help you to be more realistic in setting rules. You can learn about what's age-appropriate by reading books on child development; talking to other parents, teachers, or your pediatrician; noticing other children's skills and behavior; helping care for children on play dates; or assisting at your child's school. Learning more about the capabilities of your child's peers can help you begin to develop a sense of developmentally reasonable rules for your child. *(Rules are discussed in detail in Section Three.)*

WHY CHILDREN THINK PARENTS SHOULD SAY YES

When a child develops an inflated view of the importance of her wants and opinions, it's much harder for her to learn to get along with her family as well as with other adults and peers. Therefore, it's essential to work on reducing your child's overgrown expectations at home. If you over-apologize or act guilty when a disappointing situation arises or go too far in letting your child decide things, she will come to believe that it's your job to make her happy by saying yes to everything.

For example: Your child asks for a Popsicle and there aren't any more. If you say, "I'm really sorry we ran out of Popsicles. I'll go out to the store and get you some," she learns that she has the right to make unreasonable demands and that you will give in to them. She learns that you don't want to say no to her. It would be better to say, "I see you're disappointed. I'll put Popsicles on the shopping list next time we go to the store."

Naturally, there will also be times when you'll have to refuse to buy what she wants. This may be for many reasons – for example, perhaps it costs too much, or she has enough of them, or it's not healthy for her. In that case, it's best to let your child know not to expect you to buy her what she wants: "We're not going to buy Popsicles every week anymore, because they have too much sugar, and that's bad for your teeth."

Giving a preschooler too many choices can also lead her to believe she has the right to control any situation. For example: Mommy asks Jordan, age four, if she'll help make dinner. When Jordan says yes, Mommy asks her if she'd like to stand on her stool *or* on the chair, then if she'd like to make the salad *or* put spices on the chicken, and then if she'd like to put the pepper *or* the garlic on. This shows too much indulgence. It would be reasonable to ask if Jordan wanted to help make dinner and then ask her to do the things you feel she is capable of. Believing that the world revolves around her preferences, Jordan will likely have trouble obeying common requests like "I'd like you to wash your hands," made by her parents or by others. She would expect the adults to wait patiently as she changes her mind about whether to use the bathroom sink or the kitchen. Combining limited choices for your preschooler with confident direction provides a good balance.

HOW REQUESTS BECOME QUESTIONS

Many parents automatically phrase direct requests to their children in the form of a question: "Do you want to pick up your toys now?" "How about three more bites of chicken?" "Would you like to get in your car seat?" Preschoolers hear the question literally, think they are being offered a choice, and are likely to say no, or even "no, thank you." Not realizing that they initially phrased the request as a question, parents get annoyed and restate their unclear requests as commands: "Pick up your toys." *Children get frustrated and argue, because they believe they made a choice and it was suddenly denied.* Children may also think they have the right to refuse when directions are phrased this way: "It's almost time for bed, OK?" When you don't mean to give choices or ask your child for permission, you should say: "It's time to pick up your toys. It's nearly time for preschool." Using the "It's nearly time for…" phrase is helpful because your child learns you have a good reason behind your request, and it increases his motivation to comply so he can get to the destination or activity.

• SECTION TWO •
PITFALLS FOR PARENTS

Giving Your Child Too Much Control

WHEN PARENTS HAVE DIFFICULTY SAYING NO

Difficulties can arise when one or both parents feel bad about saying no to their children. There can be many reasons for this: not wanting to disappoint your child, wishing to avoid confrontations, wanting to treat her as an equal, or wanting her to like you, to be your friend. The busyness of daily life can make you feel guilty that you are not giving your child adequate attention. Then when you are together, you may find it hard to refuse her anything. There can be many other reasons, too – some stemming from your own childhood. Perhaps you felt your parents never listened to you, and you don't want to repeat that with your children. It is also common to have differences with your spouse about child-rearing, usually about how much say your child should have.

Some parents feel that their major goal is to make their child happy – often by saying yes to almost everything. *Parents who try too hard to please their child every day find the results disappointing.* The child is likely to end up tired, grumpy, and unappreciative of all the times she was allowed to have her way. Perhaps on a weekend outing, she is permitted to choose where to go, what treat to have, and where to eat dinner on the way home. By the end of the day, she has become even more demanding. Trying to make her happy at all costs is not the right goal. A much better day for your child is one in which you use the day's events to encourage good behavior: doing what you ask, treating people and possessions respectfully, learning about healthy foods and bodies, and knowing when and how to express her views and her feelings. These are much more useful and farsighted goals for your child. The happiness and joy your child experiences during this outing is a wonderful byproduct.

When you hesitate, express uncertainty, change your mind, or compromise – just to avoid your child's disappointment or to keep the peace – your child will get used to your giving in. Then when you *do* say no and hold to it, your child may become very frustrated and angry.

LEARNING TO COPE WITH FRUSTRATION

It is natural for children and adults to experience frustration when things don't go their way. *Parents shouldn't try to protect children from frustration, but rather should teach them how to deal with it.* You can teach them what phrases to use, how to react in an acceptable way without lashing out angrily, and what else they can do. When appropriate, you can encourage them to anticipate the time when they can have what they want: "It was frustrating that we had so little time at the park. After I put baby Kate down for her nap, we'll set up the soccer net in the yard for you. Tomorrow we can stay at the park longer."

MAINTAINING CONSISTENCY

Consistency is a difficult principle to maintain in child rearing. If you change your mind frequently, your child will test your limits more and respect your rules less – increasing your frustration as well. Making concessions can have the same effect: If you offer one cookie, your child demands two, and you agree to one and a half, or if you give in to a demand of five additional minutes of playtime beyond your time limit, you've shown your child that limit-pushing is worthwhile. That's not something we want to teach young children. Some children act as though their parents have no right to say no, and some see their parents as barriers to argue with or maneuver around, instead of as the rightful gatekeepers who have the responsibility and knowledge to guide them.

WHAT DID YOUR CHILD JUST LEARN?

You can become more consistent by keeping in mind what you want your child to learn. Perhaps your child refuses to clean up after a craft project. So as you try to get him to clean up, you negotiate, compromise with him, and wind up doing the cleanup yourself to end the arguing and the increasing frustration. Stop and remember why you told him to clean up his mess in the first place. *What did he learn in the end?* He probably learned that you didn't have the conviction that it was truly his responsibility to clean up his own mess, that arguing wears you down, and that *this is a successful tactic for him to use* to get his way in the future. These are not the lessons we want our children to learn. Looking at the situation this way helps you see what he *actually* learned. This perspective can help you to be more clear, firm, and consistent.

WHEN GIVING IN HAS GONE TOO FAR

You've gone too far in allowing your child control if she relentlessly pushes limits and demands to have decision-making power over things with which she lacks life experience. For example, if your three-year-old angrily demands pasta for dinner instead of the chicken you were making, she is showing that she has learned to expect to have as much say as you do, maybe even more. *She has learned that she's at least your "peer," or even your "parent."* Preschool-age children who have been allowed to pick the restaurant your family will eat at, choose the order of your errands, refuse to pick up toys when you ask, or talk you into changing the dinner menu have come to believe they have a lot of say.

Giving in to your child's demands encourages her continued self-centeredness. When you try to restrict her say, your child may become furious with you and with others who say no to her. Any child may act this way from time to time, but problems arise when it becomes an everyday pattern. At an extreme, by the time a child is six, she might expect to have more say than her parents in the purchase of a car and throw a tantrum in the showroom when she doesn't get her way. She has come to believe that her parents should accept her opinion and influence.

If this is a pattern, you'll need to explain to your child that there are many things parents need to decide on, and even though she may not agree, you'll be making those decisions. She may ask why you get to choose and not her. You'll have to teach her that grown-ups are the leaders and decide most things when children are little. You can explain that as she gets older, grown-ups will listen more to her opinions about the rules, even though parents are still in charge.

You can remind her what she can decide at her age. Age-appropriate choices for a preschooler include: which season-appropriate shirt she can wear, whether to have peanut-butter-and-jelly or grilled cheese for lunch, which toys to play with at home, whether to help push your shopping cart at the grocery store, and which play activity to choose at the park.

BALANCING YOUR NEEDS AND YOUR CHILD'S

Parents want to help their children feel respected and important. So it's hard to know where to draw the line between respecting your child and overindulging him. *A child whose parents inadvertently support his self-centeredness can easily develop a strong sense of entitlement, a lack of empathy for others, and a low respect for his parents' needs as well.* Frequent control conflicts with your child can make your frustration with him obvious, which can diminish his self-esteem. This is very disturbing to parents, because you want to build high self-esteem in your children.

Be sure to respect your own needs in your interaction with your child. Good parenting nurtures both the child's and parent's needs and development. Tell your child that when you have to ask him to do something over and over, it makes you frustrated and tired, and it's hard to be happy with him: "I have gotten so frustrated today having to ask you to listen so many times, it's hard for me to want to do our coloring project together." Another example of expressing your needs might be: "You're making too much noise for me, so you can stay here and find something quiet to do like a puzzle or coloring, or go to your bedroom and make noise there with the door shut."

Expressing your needs as a parent can help your child understand that other people have needs to consider. When your child's needs are always put ahead of others', he will feel that his ideas are the most important. If he complains in an elevator because another passenger pressed the button, and the parent says to the passenger, "My child really wanted to press that button," the parent is supporting the child's self-centeredness rather than

teaching him about compromise and flexibility. A better way to handle that upset child in the elevator would be to say, "That nice lady is having a turn pushing the button. Later on, we'll have a turn when others have had their turn. Let's count the floors as they light up instead."

Considering your needs, the needs of others, and the ever-present needs and demands of your child can be a difficult balance. If you feel you've given your child too much control, you'll need to work on becoming more comfortable with saying no. *Instead of giving your child maximum say now, remember that each year, your child will become increasingly ready to make more and more decisions.* You can offer increasing choices when the time is right.

BEING ASSERTIVE

Successful parenting requires that you show enough assertiveness and positive selfishness that you feel confident expressing your own needs to your child. Make sure that your child respects your needs. For example, if your child is putting her feet up on the back of your driver's seat near your head – even though she's not kicking your seat – tell her firmly to put her feet down. Don't ignore it or compromise when your child shows this kind of self-centered behavior.

WHEN PARENTS FAIL TO WORK AS A TEAM

It is not unusual for parents to have conflicts of control with their spouses as well as their children. *Parents are deeply invested in and in love with their children, and therefore feel very strongly about how to raise them.* This area can create much more conflict between them than even such central issues as where to live or how to manage their finances. Differences can emerge over many kinds of child-rearing issues such as routines and schedules, how much to expect of the children, how to punish, manners, and TV.

Working out the differences between your child-rearing approach and your spouse's can be difficult. It is hard on children when their parents have different approaches. Parents who disagree often become more extreme in their approach to compensate for their spouse's parenting style. They may become more authoritarian than they would have been if they hadn't felt the other was permissive, or more permissive to compensate for the other parent's more authoritarian approach. In many families, parents find themselves differing about whether to give in to the child's negotiation; whether reasoning with and cajoling the child is better than giving commands; or whether spanking should be used.

When parents have very different styles and have difficulty respecting each other's child-rearing approach, they may resist learning from each other instead of moving closer to each other's style and incorporating some of each other's tools. The child may then feel uncertain because he is living with conflicting rules in his home. Integrating two different parenting styles can take a long time and requires trust and confidence in each other. This is best accomplished by discussing the problems with your spouse *without* your child present, observing other families, reading parenting books, and talking to people whose opinions you both value.

Parents need to come together in their parenting goals before they can deal with specific situations. Most parents share similar goals for their children. They want to raise their kids to be confident, happy, motivated, friendly, honest, and hardworking. *Discussing goals is a good starting point for parents, because exploring each other's views on this topic is a fascinating, unifying, and low-conflict experience.* After talking over and agreeing on goals, the next step is discussing how each of you expects to help your children get to the goals. Over time, you should at least understand each other's approach.

This is the hard part. It's helpful to talk often about recent child-rearing situations that created conflict, working to understand each other's reactions and thought processes.

Most parents react to their child's behavior quickly and without a lot of thought. When you explain the reason for a parenting decision to your spouse, you are also clarifying your own logic and reasoning to yourself. These chats need to be like "show and tell," with each spouse first listening and then asking probing questions to understand one another better. Save the debate and arguing until you've listened and heard the answers to your questions.

In the following example, parents discuss their thinking concerning a recent situation in which their preschooler asked for milk with dinner, and then changed his mind and asked for juice after the milk had been poured. Mom had immediately given him the juice. Dad had told her that he disagreed with what she did.

Dad: *I felt he should drink the milk we had already given him instead of getting juice, because he needs to learn to think through his decision and not keep changing his mind.*

Mom: *I got him the juice because he's too young to know for sure what he wants, and I didn't want our dinner ruined by his crying about not getting the juice. I have awful memories of conflicts at the dinner table when I was growing up.*

Dad: *It's really OK with me if we have to have some conflict at dinner as long as we're teaching him something important. But on this issue, maybe he shouldn't get to choose at all until he's old enough to understand that what he chooses is what he gets. How old do you think that is?*

Parents can then go on to ask each other more about "why" so they can understand the underlying thinking and goals behind each other's parenting actions. This process is usually insightful and productive. After the couple has come to understand each other's views, then the debate can begin. This helps parents to gain respect for each other's methods and learn from each other so they can develop a closer collaboration as partners, and perhaps incorporate some of each other's approach into their own. Then they can feel more confident when the other parent handles child-rearing issues.

This method can help parents avoid the frustration of giving in, disagreeing or correcting each other in front of their children, or giving up and walking away. This enlightening and eventually enjoyable process helps bring couples closer together, one situation at a time, until they reach greater understanding over the years. Eventually, the couple will come to know and better trust the intent behind their spouse's child-rearing actions, and they won't need these discussions as frequently.

When parents fail to work together and learn from each other's parenting styles, their child may lose confidence in his parents' ability to set agreeable, reasonable, and firm limits and consequences. He may become increasingly challenging to raise and may begin to disrespect one or both of his parents. It's obvious to a child when his parents disagree, insult, and undermine each other. A lot of family tension arises from parents' inability to agree and to respect each other's approach to child rearing. Children need their parents to be sufficiently consistent with each other. Vocal disagreements between parents leave children aware that they can manipulate this weakness in their parents' gatekeeping. It also leaves them confused, scared, and angry.

Some parents may need professional counseling to understand the effect their very different – and maybe even opposing – parenting styles and lack of respect for each other have on their child's behavior and personality, and to learn to work together better in guiding their children's behavior.

CASE STUDY:
PLAYTIMES, BEDTIMES, AND GRUMPY KIDS

Tom and Trish had different views on the importance of regular bedtimes and evening rituals with their children, ages two and four. Tom wanted the flexibility of coming home between 6:30 and 7:30 p.m. Trish wanted a regular 8 p.m. bedtime. When Tom came home, he was hungry and needed to eat, but the children were excited to see him and wanted to play with him. He would try to eat and then play a little. He couldn't say no to the kids, so the playing started immediately and went on and on, interfering with his dinner and with the kids' bedtime. This created tension every evening. For Trish to stick to the regular bedtime, she had to become the mean one who ended the playing and fun. When Trish let it go on, the children were either overly exhausted or revved up and harder to put to sleep, and were often hard to awaken in the morning for preschool. Without enough sleep, the children were much more difficult during the day.

As Tom and Trish each explained their perspectives and needs to each other, they began to problem-solve and to look at ways that Tom could get home earlier on some nights for playtime and eat a snack in the car on the way home so he wouldn't need dinner immediately. They discussed how Tom could take over the children's bath and some of the bedtime rituals on his late nights so he had time with the kids, even though it wasn't "playtime." Tom agreed to spend more time caring for the children on the weekends so Trish could get some time off. Since the kids stayed up late on Friday nights, he could see the difference in how they behaved the day after a late night. When both parents shared the care of their grumpy children on the weekends, it became easier for Trish to allow one or two nights a week where the bedtimes were a little more flexible to accommodate Tom's later homecomings.

When parents work out their child-rearing disagreements through problem-solving discussions, as this family did, children accept limits more easily and have greater respect for both parents. The reduced tension in the home benefits the whole family.

• SECTION THREE •
GETTING BACK IN CONTROL

How to Achieve a Better Balance with Your Child

ESTABLISHING THE RULES FOR LIFE

The nature of a young child's limit-testing commonly leads to many conflicts between parents (or other caregivers) and the preschool children they nurture. As a parent, you are teaching your child important rules during her preschool years: Wash your hands with soap and warm water before you eat and after you use the toilet. Say please and thank you. Sit at the table and don't keep getting up. No turning on the television whenever you want to. You will teach your child hundreds of rules before she even begins kindergarten.

Rules are essential in teaching children the important values that you want them to eventually internalize. These internalized rules and values become part of her and help her function comfortably and successfully in her daily life, now and in her future.

Consequences are important in teaching children that they need to listen to your rules. Consequences should not be frightening, humiliating, or painful, but rather boring and tedious, and should emphasize practicing better behavior. Consequences may include time-outs, losing privileges such as TV or dessert, losing time doing something enjoyable with the parent (because the child wasted a lot of the parent's time), practicing the correct behavior, experiencing the parents' annoyance and disappointment through their words and body language, making up to the parent with an apology, or doing something nice for the parent. *The second book in this series will help you learn more about cooperation and consequences for preschoolers.*

Many parents find it hard to decide what issues to have rules about and what the rules should be. The following suggestions can guide you in rulemaking for your preschooler.

The first and most important rule is that your child needs to pay attention when you speak to her. She needs to know your expectations and rules about listening and cooperating. It's very important for parents to know what methods work best in getting cooperation at this age, such as making requests sound like fun to a preschooler. When a child doesn't listen and cooperate, she needs to know that there are consequences.

The second area of rules and limits concerns safety. For obvious reasons, it's easiest for parents to set and consistently enforce rules like not touching sharp knives, not jumping off the couch or counter, not wandering off in a crowded store, and not running into the street.

Third are the rules and limits that involve respect for other people and for possessions. They include making polite requests using "please" and "thank you," speaking respectfully and kindly instead of rudely, and listening rather than ignoring. How your child should address you – Mama or Daddy vs. your first name – and how she treats her friends and siblings also fall into this category. Preschoolers also need to learn to treat possessions – theirs, yours and others' – gently and not destructively: Use crayons only on paper, don't over-wind the music box, don't throw your blocks, don't empty the sand from your shoes onto the floor, don't throw your puzzle pieces into the toilet. Don't take others' things without asking, and don't break them or use them up.

Fourth are rules involving regular routines. Morning routines guide when the child gets dressed, eats, and gets her teeth and hair brushed, as well as getting ready for preschool or other activities. During the day, routines direct the timing of meals and snacks; playing with and helping parents; playing alone; going to the park or to see friends or go shopping; and TV time. Evening routines involve the timing and order of bedtime preparations, such as picking up toys, bath, toileting, teeth, pajamas, and in-bed time, including stories, backrubs, and chatting.

Next are rules that include the many habits children need to be taught. These include such things as dressing themselves, good behavior at the table and healthy eating habits, toileting, handwashing, getting enough physical activity, giving up pacifiers, helping with younger siblings, doing little favors for others, and controlling impulses such as not demanding a toy or treat on every trip to the store.

Last, parents need to offer opportunities and encouragement for their child to practice skills that prepare her for pre-kindergarten and kindergarten: expressing herself well when she talks; transitioning to a new activity easily, with advance notice; listening at read-aloud time and enjoying it; playing on her own for 15-minute stretches or longer; holding the pencil or crayon correctly; coloring within the lines; cutting with scissors; gluing; printing her name and other letters and numbers; learning the names and sounds of letters; and learning the names and meaning of numbers.

You want your child to absorb and internalize these rules as important habits and attitudes as she grows older. By elementary school age, your child's incorporation of these early rules will have developed into lifelong habits and values that carry the child through adulthood. Children will eventually have learned to go to bed early enough to be rested for the next day; to plan ahead so their work is done on time; to eat healthfully and exercise so they feel well; to stay within their budgets; to know how to deal with others with a balance of respect, kindness, and assertiveness; to prepare themselves for challenges, and so on. This is why it's so important to teach your child early on why you can't always say yes to her requests. **A parent needs to train a child, not cater to a child.**

USING RESPECTFUL AGE-APPROPRIATE DIRECTION

Since young children are oppositional and test limits by nature, many parents are searching for an acceptable way to enforce the rules while still showing love and respect for their children. Most parents don't want to yell or seem authoritarian: "You do it because I'm the parent!" And parents don't want to use time-outs over and over all day, keep taking privileges away, or spank their children.

A child-rearing approach called **Respectful Age-Appropriate Direction** teaches children what they need to learn without being overly permissive or authoritarian. **This practice helps children develop high self-esteem, responsibility, and empathy.** It builds their willingness to cooperate by using the following steps. First, give children advance notice when they will be required to do something. Second, make your requests to your preschooler sound enjoyable; telling children what they **can** do instead of what they can't. Third, give children

only age-appropriate choices as well as reasons for rules, expressing compassion when they're frustrated or disappointed. Fourth, when necessary, use consequences. This method makes it easier for children to cooperate. It incorporates the best strategies of child-rearing without the pitfalls of the "give your child a lot of choices and say" approach.

Respectful Age-Appropriate Direction[2] works as long as parents are careful to take the lead as gatekeepers and guides with their children.

For example, consider this exchange between a mother and her preschool daughter:

Mom: *Livia, we need to go to the post office in a few minutes to mail some packages before it closes.*

Livia: *I don't want to. I want to stay home and finish coloring my picture.*

Mom: *Honey, you can color a little longer. Then we'll go get the letter you started for Aunt Susie. You can tell me one more thing you want to say to Aunt Susie and your cousins, and we'll finish it and mail it when we go to the post office. You can put the stamp on the envelope, too. What's the last thing you're going to color?*

Livia: *The horse. And I want to tell Aunt Susie that we're going to visit her soon.*

Mom: *She'll love to hear that!*

[2] The second book in this series, **Why Do I Have To?**, teaches the skills for using **Respectful Age-Appropriate Direction** in detail. This book provides comprehensive limit-setting guidance in areas such as gaining cooperation, overcoming resistance, and using consequences that are effective for preschoolers.

In this example, the Mom gave the child advance notice, explained the time pressure, made the errand interesting, and made sure the child knew she had to cooperate and why. This shows **Respectful Age-Appropriate Direction** at its best. This approach gives the child time to stop what she's doing, know what to look forward to, and have some interest in the errand. Of course, you will still need to find ways to insist or use consequences when this approach is not enough.

WHAT TO DO WHEN RUSHED

Applying **Respectful Age-Appropriate Direction** is the goal to strive for. However, many parent/child conflicts occur when parents are rushed. It's rarely possible to practice ideal child-rearing techniques at these times, but applying some of these strategies could help. For example, consider this rushed exchange between a Mother and her preschooler:

Mom: *Adam, I just remembered I have to go to the post office and get these packages mailed before it closes. We'll have to go very quickly because it closes in 15 minutes. Run and get your shoes and I'll help you put them on.*

Adam: *I don't want to. I want to stay home and play.*

Mom: *Honey, I wish that I could have let you know ahead of time, but these packages have to go in the mail today. Go get your shoes and I'll get the boxes. If we do it really fast, then you can carry one of them into the post office and give it to the mail clerk. Let's see who can get their things first. Ready ... set ... go!*

In this example, the Mom explains what they have to do and why there is no advance notice. She finds ways to motivate her child and to help him cooperate quickly. Even in a rush, this Mom drew amazingly well on some of her best parenting tactics. Of course, she might have had to sound more insistent or even pick him up if he wasn't cooperating.

• CONCLUSION •

Watching your child develop and seeing his unique personality emerge as you help him become socialized is an incredibly rewarding and joyous experience. If you set reasonable limits for your child based on his age and ability in a manner that is appropriately firm for his personality, then you're on the right path. Throughout his childhood, you should explain the reasons behind your requests and rules. Help your child understand that his parents are his gatekeepers while he is young, that you have good reasons for your rules, and that you mean what you say. As your child gets older, you can listen more seriously to his views and let him have slowly increasing say. Respectful dialog between you and your child is important.

Reinforcing the many ways in which your preschool child learns to be a thoughtful, empathetic, and cooperative family and community member can help him see reasonable, rather than overly powerful, roles for himself. When you have successfully taught your child these roles, as well as responsibilities, you will know you did your job as a parent well, while making your years together as a family enjoyable. And you will have raised a child who is well prepared to look forward to and rise to the challenges of his future.

These guidelines can help you to lay the foundation for an approach to child-rearing that socializes your children to become enjoyable, responsible, confident, and caring members of your family and society.

ONE: *Give Your Child Age-Appropriate Choices and Say*
Learn what you can expect from your preschooler, such as how much he can understand, how the oppositional stage affects his behavior, how much he can do for himself, how long he can play alone, how well he can play with siblings and peers, and so on. Then make sure that the choices you give him are appropriate for his age rather than giving him total say in everything he does. Let him choose between two types of sandwich for lunch, what color socks to wear to school, or which acceptable video or DVD to watch during quiet time. Preschoolers should not be allowed to make decisions outside of their life experience or abilities. They should not expect to dictate where the family should go for the Sunday outing, how many cookies they can eat, or which brand of laundry detergent to buy. A young child's choices should affect only **his** life and not control your own or other people's lives. Even then, he should get only limited choices.

TWO: *Establish and Continue to Develop Limits for Your Child, in Partnership with Your Spouse*
Setting the ground rules for good life habits is essential with young children. Work with your spouse to decide which rules are important and where to set limits concerning such areas as dressing, mealtimes, bedtime, TV, and other daily routines and habits – and make them stick. Important limits also include how to treat people, animals, and possessions – and, of course, safety rules. Work with your spouse to understand the reasons behind each other's child-rearing actions to minimize spousal conflicts.

THREE: *Know That Your Child Will Test Your Limits*
Don't be surprised when your preschooler tests your best efforts to set predictable ground rules. It is natural for children to check to see if you mean what you say. Your child wants more freedom, all the time. It's just who she is as a growing person. Your job is not to give in to make your child happy, nor to avoid conflict and meltdowns by compromising. You should be helping your child to learn to do what you ask by being confident and firm.

FOUR: *Just Because Children Push Limits Doesn't Mean the Rules Should Be Broken*
Your child will try to break the rules to suit himself and make demands and unreasonable requests. But you should not convey that most rules are open for negotiation and compromise. Your child is not your peer. He needs to know that you mean what you say, that you have good reasons behind your rules, and that you won't cave in when he tests your limits. Giving in teaches your child that your rules and limits can be broken if he bothers you long or loudly enough about it. Remember, consistency is important.

FIVE: *Don't Phrase Requests as Questions*
Your child will hear your request as a choice if you say: "Can you pick up your toys now?" or "It's time for bed, OK?" To a preschooler, these phrases have an obvious answer: "No." Be direct and firm: "It's time to pick up your toys now," or "Let's go get your books and put on your PJs so we can read your bedtime stories."

SIX: *Make It Fun for Your Child to Cooperate*
Learn good ways to get cooperation without constantly butting heads with your child. Your preschooler will give you more cooperation when you make your request sound fun – tell her what she can do, instead of only what she can't. For example: "Let's get a paper cup and poke some holes in it to take into your bath." Or: "If you pick up your toys quickly, there'll be enough time for you to help me cook." Using this "make it fun" technique is an excellent way to get better cooperation from your young pre-logical-aged child.

continued on page 38

• GUIDELINES FOR SETTING HEALTHY LIMITS FOR YOUR CHILD •

SEVEN: *Help Your Child Understand the Reasons Behind Your Rules*

Giving your child reasons helps him to understand why you have the rule. Knowing your reasons will encourage children to be more cooperative and respectful, and even to be better thinkers and problem-solvers.

EIGHT: *Develop a Set of Consequences*

Consequences teach a child not to keep repeating misbehavior and help her behave in a more socialized fashion. Parents should avoid consequences that frighten, hurt, or humiliate, and instead should emphasize boring and tedious consequences, with an emphasis on practicing better behavior. Besides time-outs, these may include losing time from a favorite activity, practicing the correct behavior, and simply facing parents' displeasure.

NINE: *Respond to Your Child's Angry Comments*

Your child's frustrated and angry feelings can be heard when he says things like: "You're a bad Mommy." "I'm not going to be your friend." "I don't have to do what you say." It is reasonable to allow your child to say he is angry at you and why. Do not allow him to be rude. Help him to understand himself better by saying, "You don't like it when Mommy says no." Tell him "It's not OK to say mean things to me. But, Ben, you can say, 'I'm mad. I don't like it when we have to leave the playground.' "

TEN: *Listen to Your Child's Views*

Although your child may become angry and say hurtful things when you say no, give her a chance to calm down, and listen to what she has to say. But make it clear that you're not promising to change your decision, and help her understand what she has to do next. Talk to her about the situation in a manner that helps her realize she has been heard and understood.

Dad: *I can see that you're mad at me because I can't let you keep playing now.*

Abby: *I want to play in my room. I don't want to go to preschool.*

Dad: *Some days it's hard to stop playing and go to school. Some days it's hard for me to go to work. Let's get dressed and have breakfast, because Teacher Sarah and I want you to hear the first story at preschool.*

ELEVEN: *Develop Thoughtful Decision-Making with Your Child*

Help your child to see that he can decide on more things as he gets older. Practice thoughtful decision-making with him by having him explain the reasons behind his decisions to you.

Parent: *I know you want to stay outside and play some more, but it's getting dark outside. Tell me why it's a good idea for you to keep playing outside when it's very hard to see anything.*

Make sure that your child knows that although you're interested in his thinking, you will still make the final decision because that's the job of a parent.

TWELVE: *Encourage Empathy*

Your child needs to understand that her words and actions affect you and others, and that she needs to consider whether she's inconveniencing, annoying, upsetting, or angering you or other people. When your child is shouting, "I don't like your idea! I want to do it my way! My way is better!" you can say, "When people tell me that I don't have good ideas, it hurts my feelings and makes me mad. Then I don't want to play or do things with that person. You'll need to say that a different way." Make sure you are assertive and selfish enough as a parent that your preschooler doesn't feel the world revolves around her.

B. ANNYE ROTHENBERG, Ph.D., *author,* has been a child/parent psychologist and a specialist in child rearing and development of young children for more than 20 years. Her parenting psychology practice is in Emerald Hills, California. She is also an adjunct clinical assistant professor of pediatrics at Stanford University School of Medicine. Dr. Rothenberg was the founder/director of the Child Rearing parenting program in Palo Alto, California, and is the author of the award-winning book *Parentmaking* and other parenting education books for parenting guidance professionals. She is the mother of one son.

MARION ELDRIDGE, *illustrator,* has been a professional illustrator for 20 years, developing a unique, warm, and whimsical style. She has illustrated numerous children's books for a variety of publishers and has also created illustrations for children's magazines, greeting card companies, and UNICEF. She teaches at the New Hampshire Institute of Art. Marion lives with her husband in Billerica, Massachusetts, and is the mother of one daughter. Her website is www.marioneldridge.com.

ACKNOWLEDGMENTS

The author wishes to thank **SuAnn** and **Kevin Kiser** for their outstanding critiques and collaboration on the Children's Story and **Sharon Barela** and **Caroline Grannan** for their excellent editing of the Parents' Guide. **Cathleen O'Brien** has done a remarkable job on book design. The feedback provided by the parents in the focus groups at the *Playschools* in Atherton and Redwood City; *Merry Moppet Preschool in Belmont*; and *St. Matthias Preschool* and *Our Place Child Care Center* in Redwood City, all in California, was very helpful and appreciated. Gratitude is expressed for the very useful reviews by the following pediatricians, all of whom are parents of preschoolers: *Andrea Enright*, M.D.; *Amy Oro*, M.D.; *Kerstin Rosen*, M.D.; and *Linda Strain*, M.D.

"For years, Dr. Annye Rothenberg has been a wise and treasured resource in our San Francisco Peninsula region to the many families she has counseled as well as to the guidance professionals whom she mentors. **She has written a marvelous book that I highly recommend.** I am delighted that her wisdom and experience will now be shared with a broader audience."
— Mary Ann Carmack, MD, PhD, Chair, Department of Pediatrics, Palo Alto (CA) Medical Clinic

"If you're tired, frustrated, and at your wits' end over a preschooler who throws tantrums, ignores you, interrupts, and otherwise threatens your sanity, **you need this book!** Dr. Rothenberg's practical advice enabled us to transform our cranky, fitful four-year-old into a confident, loving child."
— Jessie and Andy Chan, Parents of three children (ages 4, 8 and 13)

"This is exactly the type of children's book I've been waiting for! Dr. Rothenberg has given parents an exceptional tool to use with their children that includes a fantastic parenting guide. **This is a book that as a preschool director I will recommend to all my parents."**   — Marlene Coe, Director, Playschool, Redwood City, CA

"Brilliant and very practical!"
— Barbara B. LeBlanc, MSW, LCSW, Director, The Parenting Center at Children's Hospital, New Orleans

"This combination children's book/parents' guide offers an entertaining story with a new perspective for preschoolers, while providing clear and practical parenting guidance. **Both will have a very useful impact on families."**
— Linda Lisi Juergens, Executive Director, National Association of Mothers' Centers, Levittown, NY

"This delightful children's book clearly illustrates, from a child's perspective, **why a parent saying no is sometimes the quickest way to true self-esteem."**   — Peggy Spear, Editor, Bay Area Parent magazine

"This concise and complete guide should be **required reading by any parent who wishes to foster a healthy and happy family."**
— Suzanne M. Einsiedl, RN, MSN, Pediatric Nurse Practitioner and mother of three

"This book is a wonderful resource for families and caregivers of young children. The playful children's story helps preschoolers see the world beyond their immediate needs, and the practical parents' guide explains preschoolers' development and needs while teaching how to establish appropriate expectations and limits."
— Elizabeth Stillwell, M Ed, Director, Early Childhood Center at Cornell University

"This book helped us re-evaluate and refocus the way we guide our children. **What a great resource!"**
— Dana and Brian Ascher, Parents of a four-year-old and a toddler

" 'Amen,' I say after reading Annye Rothenberg's children's story and parents' guide. **This work will strengthen the self-esteem of both parent and child."**
— Carol Kaplan-Lyss, MAT, Parenting Educator and Counselor, Family Center, Clayton, MO

"Dr. Rothenberg's book fills a great gap in library collections. In an engaging style, it gives insight for both children and their parents on dealing with the common issue of 'having it my way'."
— Melinda Wing, Head Librarian, Palo Alto (CA) Children's Library

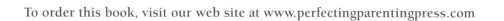
To order this book, visit our web site at www.perfectingparentingpress.com